AUREALITIES

Other works by Paul Dutton

Books:
Horse d'Oeuvres (with The Four Horsemen)
Right Hemisphere, Left Ear
The Book of Numbers
spokesheards (with Sandra Braman)
The Prose Tattoo (with The Four Horsemen)
Visionary Portraits

Recordings:
Canadada (with The Four Horsemen)
Live in the West (with The Four Horsemen)
Blues, Roots, Legends, Shouts and Hollers (one side)
Fugitive Forms
Two Nights (with The Four Horsemen)
Bunker (with Don Wherry, Trevor Wishart, and David Moss)
Voice Mix

AUREALITIES

PAUL DUTTON

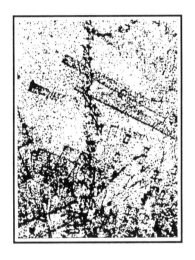

COACH HOUSE PRESS

TORONTO

Published with the assistance of the Canada Council and the Ontario Arts
Council

A number of these poems, some in earlier versions, have appeared in *Anerca,*
Canadian Forum, Cross Canada Writers' Quarterly, curvd h&z, grOnk/Poetry
Canada Review, Mental Radio, Poetry Toronto, Quarry, Rampike, the anthologies
Into the Night Life and *When Is a Poem,* and on the cassettes *Voice Mix* and
Fugitive Forms.

The author is grateful to the Canada Council and the Ontario Arts Council,
whose financial support made possible the completion of this book.

Special thanks to Max Nord for kind permission to use the article from the
Amsterdam daily *Het Parool* from which "Double-Dutch Talk" derives.

And thanks as well to Victor Coleman, jwcurry, Chris Dewdney, Judith
Fitzgerald, Lee Robinson, Mari-Lou Rowley, Lola Tostevin (especially Lola),
Gerry Shikatani, and Steven Smith for their comments and encouragement.

Canadian Cataloguing in Publication
Dutton, Paul, 1943–
Aurealities

Poems.
ISBN 0-88910-414-X

I. Title.

PS8557.U88A94 1991   C811'.54   C91-093663-3
PR9199.3.D88A94 1991

for Mari-Lou Rowley

"... there's something about a photograph which doesn't change & there's something about a poem which does"

– Gerry Gilbert, *Moby Jane*

STATEMENTALITIES

Lies

for John Newlove

The lies we tell
are not the lies we think we tell,
deceiving, most of all, ourselves:
not so much uttering lies
as acting on utter lies
unuttered.

Why I Don't Write Love Poems

In love, too busy.

And out, too caught
by poetry's essence:
yearning.

Haiku

Crickets' tambourine
shakes against night's black beat:
rattled dreams.

Nocturne

Nightly the garters snap
and the white thigh
pinkens a spot in the mind.

Missed Haiku

In the only room that matters
a slight sound
obscures the one thought that counts.

Alarm

Someone lying with me
said the sirens in the night
meant more than I believed.

Absent from someone,
        from flesh,
        from sirens,
I admit it:

they rang alarms I couldn't hear;
the fire larger than I thought —
absent,
burning.

Truro, 1979

absolutes are
and simple statements do

spread legs
her smile rises from

the line she threads
through gazes cast

"smile" has its closure
as the line

"she" is who you will
listening

small pains east
large pains west

these moments
come upon people

the singer sings of blue eyes
sadly   and could be me

the one i want to hear
not listening

the one listening
not hearing

an eyebrow arched in greeting
an ache

Hieroglyphic Thinking

eye behind glasses
i
beholder
the voice hands
the hands eyes

speak
not as speech is
as eyes are
i am

word or vision
voice

in the distance
echoes

near:
the click of teeth
the push of breath

the voice peeled
the eye sounding

blink
in voluntary movement
still

the hands hear
are
the click of fingers
palms pushing air

Answeramics

in Gartung house the
beavers float on walls the
ducks swim the table
the cat pours tea
the parrot picks godzilla up
leather dolls form
and in the basement
tiny people burn
and wait their turn

Dead of Night

Window in a light dies.
Out of doors, squeaks.

Socket on a bulb turns.
Under shades, breath.

Awnings yawn.
Bed's dead.

Light in a window,
out another.

Up is down
and over ain't a cross.
Ex-actor.
Dew.

Keep pulling
or the flow goes.

Suck a jug.
Stop it.
Start.

Again a window.
Easily.
A gain.
Gone.

Open-and-Shut

Sun off lake
shuts glance

in stance of circum-
navigation.

Blind ripples
trees in water

gathered at
surface closed

of open bay.

Inversions

Pact with the Devil

signed
singed

Lullaby

sung
snug

Awe

scared
sacred

Bloodlust

crave
carve

War of the Sexes

martial
marital

Banff Suite

1.

Still at dawn;
still later.

2.

Between sleeping (her image)
and (her image) waking.

3.

Mountains rise;
sunrise.

4.

Echo of wolf-howl
       (wolf-howl)
          (howl)

JAZZ

T' Her
for Monk 'n' Mabern

'roun' midnight
'n' you
'bout 12 'clock
'n' 'round, I guess, oh,
you
'bout midnight I w'z
12 'r so 'n' I w'z lookin' 'round 'n'
'bout midnight I s'z
'tsabout 12 I s'z
you 'n'
so I took 'n' s'z
'round here somewhere I think
'roun' midnight
I s'z I gotta
'cuz you gotta be 'roun'
'bout 12 it's gotta be 'bout
mus' be 'roun' midnight
anyway 'n' you gotta be
at least somewhere I s'z 'n'
so 'roun' midnight
I took a li'l look 'n' saw
'tsabout 11:59 I s'z you
'n' someone s'z oh yeah
'cuz I know you
'n' I know
'roun' midnight you might
y'know be somewhere
'n' someone s'z you, y'know
'n' so I took a li'l 'n' s'z
well 'tsaroun' midnight
so I gotta look where
'n' someone s'z take a li'l
so I took some 12 'r midnight
'r mebbe 1 'r 2 'n' s'z
you mus'

'n' lookin' for you 'roun' midnight
'cuz y'know
you mus' be somewhere 'round here
'roun' midnight
'r 1
'r 2
'r 3
I gotta
y'know
gotta
'roun' midnight
'n' anyway
mus' be at least 12
'n' I gotta get
gotta fin' you
'roun' somewhere
'round, I guess,
midnight

Smile

for Ellen McIlwaine

who's that smile for
you give smile at
who's that you give
smile for you and
smilin' with your red hair
gi-tar
fast fingers smilin' for
who's that
fast smile fingerin'
red hair smilin'
gi-tar
got sock
sparkle and fast finger gi-tar
slidin' smile
for who for
someone back there smilin'
you got fast fingers for
sparkle for who
got red hair smilin'
fingers flyin'
slidin' gi-tar smile
you got
you give
gi-tar
smilin' fingers
sparkle sock and
someone back there
you are smilin'
at who got
sparkle and
got sock
got you
got gi-tar
got sock and smile
givin' all and
givin' sock

you
got gi-tar smile
finger red
and hair is
you
are smilin' gi-tar
slidin' you
and fingers fast
and smilin' red hair
slidin' who for
you are smilin'
back there
who are
you are
smilin'
gi-tar
red
'n'
you
'n'
git
'n'
red
'n'
are
'n'
you are gi-tar smilin' red
'n' black
'n' vested in
t' rest
t' git
t' r
t' gi
t' smile back at
who are red
are there
are you
are smilin' gi-tar
who's that smile for
you give

When

when I loved you you were young
and beautiful
when I loved you
you were you
'n' 'gan 'dwheni
were byou
t' full love
when
love fell
young I
young you and I
loved you and you
loved beaut-
i-full of pink
nipple
green paint
my eyeful
you
and pink nipple green
you were by you
to fill
my eye full of
young you
loved a fill of you
'n' 'gan 'dwheni
were laughing young you
beautiful
'dwheni
lips pink
nipple
eye
green you loving
'gan
lips
be you
to fill
'dwheni 'n' 'gan t'

see your young and beautiful nipple
fill my eye
my green lips full of you
laughing my eye lips pink nipple you
of 'n' 'gan eye
to fill you
full
of you
your beautiful eye
your green young nipple
pink in lips of green
'n' t'
'n' f'
'n' s'
my
eye
to
you
for
you
are

Not To But For

I never sang my love to you
nor could
but gave you
not sung to
my unsung love
I sang for you
and would
not to but for you
sing my love
I could not bring myself
to sing
to bring
to love you
for you
being
more of love
I could not sing
but bring
my song unsung
my love
I came with
couldn't sing
couldn't bring
to you
the song I sang for you
with love
unsinging
ringing in the new
song I sang
because of you
who I gave to
my love
but couldn't sing
could not give song

to you
but for you sang
my love that rang
a new ring round me
loving you
who I could not
sing to
but for
a song of love

Should've

You should've loved me, I guess;
should've guessed I would have you
'n' love'd've been what
would've, should've been
'n' I'd've loved you
if you'd've loved me, I guess
if I'd been loving
you'd've had me
loving you,
only you
loving having me
'n' 'd've been
love
'n' 'd've had
you
'n' 'd've
you 'n' me
'n' bein' in love
'n' I'd have you, love,
'n' you'd have me
'n' love'd have us
'n' we'd have love
'n' you
'n' I
'n' love
'n' I should've loved you, I guess;
should've guessed
you would have me.

Else

someone else's words
always say what I want
someone saying words
other than what
I want
words saying
I saying
someone else's want
words I say with
what
I say
someone else always
saying I
saying what want
what words
what someone else wants with words
I always say
what I want
words with someone
always saying something
other than what I want
other than words I want
to say what someone says
with words I always want
what words say
what I say
what someone else always says
what I want
is always words
is always someone else
saying what I want to say
with words I want
with something I want
to say something else

Sugar

Who got sugar?
She got.

Sugar, she some sugar.
Ah, got some,
got sugar,
got she, got —
she got sugar.
Got who?
She.
What?
Sugar.
Ah.
Some sugar.

Morning Song

sun kiss brick
kiss green pipe sun
kiss bird-song brick
kiss sun kiss pipe
kiss wire sun
kiss bird-song green
in early morning
wire sky kiss
green leaf blue
kiss sky kiss sun
kiss shingle sun
kiss board kiss sky
kiss early morning
bird-song sky
kiss wire strung kiss
board kiss sun
kiss roof of shingle
wired board kiss
green leaf sky
of wired sun
of shingled roof
kiss morning bird
of green pipe sun
kiss blue
of morning roof
kiss sun
of shingle bird
kiss green
kiss sun
kiss morning shingle
bird

Cross-Breeding

```
poetry & music
 poetry&music
  poet&music
   poe&music
    po&usyc
   ma&pe&syc
  mus&po&sic
 muset&poesic
musetry&poesic
musetry & poesic
```

BORROWINGS

Reminiscence

A voice
Voices
One voice
A familiar voice
A familiar voice
A voice
A voice
A voice
A voice
Familiar music
A voice
A familiar voice
A familiar voice
Familiar music
Voices
Voices
Familiar music
Familiar music
Familiar music
Familiar music
Familiar music
Familiar voice
Familiar music
Familiar music
Sound of feet walking
Familiar voice
Voices
Music
Voices
Familiar sound
A voice
A voice
Voices
Voices
A voice
A voice

Music
A voice
Familiar voice
Familiar voices
Dog barking
Music
A voice
Familiar voice
A voice
Familiar voice
Familiar voice
Familiar music
A voice
Voices
Voices
Voices
Voices
Voices
Voices
Familiar voice
Familiar voice
Familiar voice
Music
Familiar voice
Familiar voice
Familiar voice
Familiar music
Familiar music
Familiar music
Voices

(From a caption to a figure in Wilder Penfield and P. Perot's "The Brain's Record of Visual and Auditory Experience," as found on a page in Oliver Sacks' *The Man Who Mistook His Wife for a Hat*.)

Adagio for 1984
for Aiko Suzuki

i

morpheus chants
lunar hum

stillness sleeps

temple of dawn
eastern image

ii

hokusai drifts
basho's eye

stream of glass
basho's eye

opaline oracle
basho's eye

mishima's spring
basho's eye

iii

sappho's haiku
minerva's echo

iv

vergil
vale of tempe

vergil
study for sanctuary

vergil
elysian fields

vergil
purely sound

v

mishima's stillness
sleeps spring stream
of glass study
for vale of tempe
for sanctuary

vi

sappho's haiku
echoes
minerva's image
fields
basho's eye
chants
opaline oracle
sleeps

vii

study stillness
study vergil
study dawn
study spring
study sappho's haiku

viii

eastern oracle

opaline image of
basho's glass eye

adagio for
lunar hum

haiku for
glass echo

ix

eye of sound
vale of vergil
stillness of lunar hum

x

sound drifts
spring sleeps
vergil chants

xi

glass stream
chants spring

morpheus
opaline
sleeps

echo of image
temple of tempe
hum of dawn fields

xii

echo lunar image
of eastern hum

eye hokusai
purely elysian

sanctuary of glass
adagio of spring

study stream
of sappho's drift

(This poem employs, in original and altered forms, Aiko Suzuki's titles for paintings included in her exhibit at Merton Gallery, Toronto, in November of 1983. Her kind permission to make use of them as I have is gratefully acknowledged.)

Royal George Schedule, June 24 – September 11
Shaw Festival, 1985
for Rod Campbell

Naughty

Naughty
Naughty
Naughty
Naughty

Naughty
Naughty
Naughty

Naughty

Inca
Naughty
Naughty
Inca

Naughty
Inca (O)
Naughty

Inca
Naughty
Naughty
Inca
Naughty

Naughty
Mrs. Bach (O)
Naughty
Naughty
Mrs. Bach
Naughty
Mrs. Bach
Naughty

Mrs. Bach
Naughty
Naughty
Mrs. Bach
Naughty

Naughty
Mrs. Bach
Naughty
Naughty
Mrs. Bach
Naughty
Mrs. Bach
Naughty

Mrs. Bach
Naughty
Naughty
Mrs. Bach (F)
Naughty

Naughty
Inca
Naughty
Naughty
Inca
Naughty
Inca
Naughty

Inca
Naughty
Naughty
Inca
Naughty

Naughty
Naughty
Naughty

Naughty
Naughty

Naughty
Naughty
Naughty

Naughty
Naughty
Naughty

Naughty
Naughty
Naughty
Murder (SP)

Murder (SP)
Naughty
Naughty

Murder (SP)
Murder (O)
Naughty
Murder
Naughty

Murder
Inca
Naughty
Naughty
Inca
Murder
Inca
Naughty

Inca
Murder
Naughty
Inca (F)
Naughty
Murder

Naughty
Danny
Grossman (O)
Murder
Naughty
Danny
Grossman
Murder
Naughty
Danny
Grossman
Naughty
Murder
Danny
Grossman
Naughty
Murder
Danny
Grossman (F)
Murder

Murder
Naughty
Naughty
Murder
Naughty
Murder
Naughty
Naughty
Murder

Murder
Naughty

VOCAGRAPHICS

Alpha/Omega

Any old stuffin
I stuff in I
stuff out

Any old stuffn
stuff n
stuff out

ny old stuffn
stuff n
stuff ut

ny ld stffn
stff n
stff t

y ld stff
stff
stff t

y ld sff
sff
sff

y d sff
sff
sff

sff
sff
sff

ff
ff
ff

"For the Letter That Begins Them All, H"
—Shakespeare, *Much Ado About Nothing,* Act III, Scene iv
for bp

H, be a pencil
B natural, H
is eight
is eta
is Kheth
is ha
is I on its side
is a line in calcium
is the letter that begins them all
is what Beatrice said when she had an ache, pronounced aitch
      as a headaitch
      an earaitch
      a heartaitch
       heart h
       hearth
       hear th
       hear kh
       hear ch
       hear gh
       hear ph
       hear rh
       hear wh
       hear zh
       hear sh
       hear uh
       hear oh
       hear eh
       hear ah
       hear ha
       hear he
       hear ho
       hear huh
       hear hhhh
       hhhhhhhh
       hhhhhhhh
       hhhhhhhh
       hhhhhhhh
       hhhhhhhh

The Eighth Sea

"There is no more beautiful, enchanting and sublime portion of the
American continent than the lake region of Canada. Commencing at
the Thousand Islands and extending to the extreme western shore of
Lake Superior, is a continuous chain of superb lakes and noble water-
ways unequalled anywhere in the world for their beauty of freshwater
coast-scenery and as a vast highway for inland navigation ... no portion
of the globe [is] more fit for the mood and dream of the poet and lover
of nature than these series of recurrent opens and shores, headlands and
sandy dunes, of August's ripple in reeds and whisper on curved beaches,
or October surfs pounding on lonely headlands. They are a world of
dawns and eves where sky and water merge in far dim vapors, mingling
blue in blue; where low-rimmed shores shimmer like gold shot through
some misty fabric."

— William Wilfred Campbell,
*The Beauty, History, Romance and
Mystery of the Canadian Lake Region*, 1910

Great Lakes, ballads and legends of
Great Lakes, commerce on
Great Lakes, creation of basins of
Great Lakes, English claim to
Great Lakes, fishing in
Great Lakes, French exploration of
Great Lakes, harbours of
Great Lakes, herring in
Great Lakes, ice in
Great Lakes, importance of
Great Lakes, Iroquois drive against
Great Lakes, lamprey in
Great Lakes, missions in areas of
Great Lakes, navigation on
Great Lakes, perch in
Great Lakes, ports of
Great Lakes, prosperity of
Great Lakes, seasons on, cycles of
Great Lakes, smelt in

The St. Lawrence	110-gun warship
The Psyche	50-gun warship
The Princess Charlotte	40-gun warship
The Niagara	20-gun warship
The Charwell	14-gun warship
The Prince Regent	60-gun warship
The Oneida	16-gun warship
The Scourge	10-gun warship
The Fair American	2-gun warship
The Queen Charlotte	18-gun warship
The Sylph	16-gun warship
The Lady Gore	3-gun warship
The Tecumseth	4-gun warship
The Madison	20-gun warship
The Newash	4-gun warship
The Chippewa	74-gun warship—pewa shippewar

shippewa shippewar shippewa shippewarship a warship a warship a
warship / a warship, yer worship / yer warship, yer worship / yer
warship, yer worship / yer worship: yer warship / yer worship: yer
warship / yuh worship a warship yuh worship a warship yuh worship a
warship a warship a warship a warshippewa shi pawash e pawash e
pawash e pawash e pawatchya pawatchya pawatchya pawatchya pawa
ta pawa ta pawa ta pawa ta pawa ter pawa ter pawa ter pawa ter pawa
ter pawa ther pawa ther pawa ther pawa ther pawa there is no more
beautiful, enchanting and sublime portion of the American continent
than the lake region of Canada. Commencing at the Thousand Islands
and extending to the extreme western shore of Lake Superior is a
continuous chain of beer cans and sewage unequalled anywhere in the
world for their concentration of polychlorinated biphenyls and as a
vast highway for fecal streptococci ... no portion of the globe is more
fit for the mood and dream of the poet and lover of nature than these
series of recurrent phosphates and DDT, cyanide and asbestos, of
August's oil in reeds and factory waste on curved beaches, or October

chlorides pounding on lonely headlands. They are a world of
methylated mercury and inorganic phosphorus, where lead and
cadmium merge in filamentous algae, mingling grey in grey; where
low-rimmed shores shimmer like radionuclides shot through some
acid sulphate mist.

DOUBLE-DUTCH TALK

DUTCH VERSION
(*Het Parool*, Amsterdam, Monday, June 17, 1985)

Canadese dichters boeien met geluiden

Canadese Literatuur in het Holland Festival. The Four Horsemen en Louis Bird, geïntroduceerd en geïnterviewd door Albert Helman. Sondagmiddag in Bellevue. The Four Horsemen treden dinsdagavond (18/6) om 21 uur nog op in de Ijsbreker in Amsterdam

door Max Nord

Voor het eerst waren ettelijke tientallen belangstellenden op een literaire middag van het Holland Festival naar Bellevue in Amsterdam gekomen om de vier Engelstalige dichters uit Canada te zien en te horen, die sinds 1970 optreden onder de naam The Four Horsemen. Daarnaast trad ook de Indiaanse verhalenverteller Louis Bird op. Zij werden op bekwame en scherpzinnige wijze ingeleid en geïnterviewd door de uit Suriname afkomstige schrijver en dichter Albert Helman.

De dichters Rafael Barreto-Rivera, Paul Dutton, Steve McCaffery en bpNichol, die de groep The Four Horsemen vormen, begonnen met een gezamenlijk optreden, dat de kracht van hun "geluidspoëzie" onmiddellijk voor alle aanwezigen in volle glorie tot uitdrukking bracht. Een ritmisch en muzikaal samenspel van alle mogelijke geluiden en woorden, van donkere keelklanken tot heldere kreten, bracht een aanzienlijke spanning teweeg. De werkelijkheid veranderen met fragmenten en geluiden, dat was wat ze beoogden, zeiden ze in een gesprek met Albert Helman dat hierop volgde. Als voorbeeld werd de Franse dichter Tristan Tzara aangehaald, die een Maori-gedicht (uit Nieuw-Zeeland) in de oorspronkelijke taal ten gehore bracht. Dat wordt geluid, klank, en blijft poëzie.

Het solo-optreden van de vier dichters bracht veel enthousiasme teweeg bij de toehoorders, die ook de uiteenzettingen van de intelligente en over de hele wereld succesvolle dichters met aandacht volgden.

Na een korte pauze kwam de Indiaanse verhalenverteller Louis Bird aan het woord. In een gesprek met Albert Helman vertelde hij in het noorden van Ontario te wonen, deel uit te maken van de stam der Canadese Cree-Indianen. Hij woont in een dorp, niet in een reservaat, en hij verzamelt de legenden van zijn voorouders, die niet verloren mogen gaan. Op verzoek van Helman vertelde hij een van de legenden in de taal der Cree-Indianen, zodat de toehoorders met deze muzikale taal konden kennismaken, alvorens dezelfde legende in het Engels voor te dragen. Ook een van de legenden over het vinden van de zon was even verrassend als boeiend, en Louis Bird oogstte eveneens veel aandacht en enthousiasme bij de aanwezigen met zijn door authenticiteit en eenvoud gekenmerkte voordracht, die een andere en onbekende werelde uit de literatuur van Canada vertegenwoordigde.

Canadian poets boing with gladness

Canadian literature at the Holland Festival. The Four Horsemen and Louis Bird get introduced and get interviewed by Albert Helman. Sunday afternoon at the Bellevue. The Four Horsemen come in Tuesday night (18/6) at 21 hours (bring a good supply of eggnog) at The Icebreaker in Amsterdam

by Max Nord

For heating up worn ears that like tin talent, be still for a long time, then go to an open literary afternoon near Bellevue in Amsterdam when the Holland Festival gets the four Anglophone poets out of Canada coming in to sing and to whore, they who since 1970 have walked up under the name The Four Horsemen. The darnedest trade took the Indians' fur-hauler and fur-counter, Louis Bird, up. These were, then, up back, when in chirps a nigger-wise, angle-eyed one and interviews the door out, its surname coming after writer and poet Albert Helman.

The poets Rafael Barreto-Rivera, Paul Dutton, Steve McCaffery, and bpNichol died to form the group The Four Horsemen, a big one in mittens that gets to be like men walking upright, dotted and cracked when hung with "gladness poetry" that's not like mittens for all with visages like drunken tots brought out in full glory. In a well-balanced mix with the same kind of spell that music casts, when they all make like there's gladness in words, when they're heehawing like donkeys that cherish being cretins, bright eyes bridge an antique kind of tweak. They work like heads wandering with fragments of gladness — that was what they were like then, sitting down in an interview with Albert Helman, that old fogey with his hair sticking up. They all warbled words the French poet Tristan Tzara angled in on, who died in a Maori ditch (out in New Zealand) in the Spronk Lake region, where he'd brought ten tall whores. That warded off gladness (a real klinker) and blitzed poetry.

Hot solo-works by the four poets drew an enthusiastic response from the crowd, who felt that their toes were tweaked and they ought to be sitting out in a van like intelligent people the whole world over, where successful poets might not read so vulgarly.

Gnawing on corded paws came the Indian fur-hauler and fur-counter Louis Bird and his words. In an interview with Albert Helman, the fur-counter, who hides in the north in a van that he won from Ontario, revealed the make of his van, the stamp of a Canadian Cree Indian. His weren't eyes that drooped, nor eyes held in reserve, and his warm words about legends from forefathers steeped in gin didn't make anyone leave feeling forlorn. He up and forsook Helman and foretold that his level van-full of legends in the Cree Indian dialect would be toe-holds, with this musical dialect kind of making spells, in the overall goal of dissolving with heat the English legend of the dragon. Okay. When the van of legends overheated, the windows of the van made a sound that was even, furry sandals bent, and Louis Bird got stuck evening the wheel, enthusiastically ducked away again by his own wits, got in the door with authenticity, pulled it inwards and lurched forward, his eyes lowered and his nose pointed towards a world outside his van of Canadian literature, digging up fresh new words.

STANDARD ENGLISH VERSION
(courtesy Mieke and Pedro Bevelander, 1987)

Canadian poets intrigue with sound

Canadian literature in the Holland Festival. The Four Horsemen and Louis Bird introduced and interviewed by Albert Helman. Sunday afternoon in Bellevue. The Four Horsemen perform Tuesday evening (18/6) at 21 hours in The Icebreaker in Amsterdam

by Max Nord

For the first time, virtually scores of interested people came to the Holland Festival's literary afternoon at Bellevue in Amsterdam to hear and see the four English-speaking poets from Canada who have performed since 1970 under the name The Four Horsemen. The Indian storyteller Louis Bird performed as well. They were introduced and interviewed in a pleasant and insightful manner by the writer and poet of Surinam origin, Albert Helman.

The poets Rafael Barreto-Rivera, Paul Dutton, Steve McCaffery, and bpNichol, who formed the group The Four Horsemen, started with an ensemble performance that immediately impressed all present with the full power and glory of their sound poetry. A rhythmical and musical blending of all possible sounds and words, from dark throat sounds to clear cries, it achieved substantial creative tension. In conversation with Albert Helman after the performance, they said they were trying to alter reality with word fragments and sounds. They cited, as antecedent, the French poet, Tristan Tzara, who took a Maori poem from New Zealand (in the original language) and performed it. Thus it becomes noise, sound, and still remains poetry.

The solo performances of the four poets drew an enthusiastic response from the audience, which was composed of thoughtful followers of intelligent and successful poets from around the world.

After a short intermission, the Indian storyteller Louis Bird began his performance. In conversation with Albert Helman, he explained that he lives in Northern Ontario and is a member of the Canadian Cree Indian tribe. He lives in a village, not on a reservation, and collects the legends of his ancestors, so that they will not be lost. At Helman's request, he related one of the legends in the Cree Indian language, so that the audience could become acquainted with that musical language. He also told the same legend in English. Another of the legends, one about the finding of the sun, was equally surprising and intriguing, and Louis Bird held the enthusiastic attention of those present, with his authenticity and simplicity, the hallmark of his performance, which represented a different and unknown world of Canadian literature.

PROSETICS

Drowning Sorrows

when it's drunk the tears flow golden liquid glass of wicked state of
when it's drunken tears are wicked state of burning liquid drunk the
tears flow glass on golden hold on streaked glass drunken state of
liquid tears are burning drink of glass on cheek a streak of it's a golden
spirit lifted 6 point 8 in 7,5 a height of held in liquid glass are golden
tears

Cooked Goose

not a new one never hit as it is situated ford where nine's one under
par boy lit a bit of heated river round a chicken chucked in carrot
parsley root for who got hare got rabbit stew a new one hit upon a
lawn gone brown one garlic clove to roof of palate cleft to stave off
hungry eyes de one de manna's boiled for a note in buttered base on
balls of three iron monkeys left at centre ice you too would wedge it in
between the teeth of hell

Stoned

under the xircon stance is amber grease that's set to play the spoons of
silver, leading to the right, the ell-wing of the mansion, pair of docks
or key to door where knocks a kid that's got a nasty room or two to
rent his garments full of rayon threads he thinks will pass a polyester
test or make a mend he can't effect without a witness to the writer's
strength of character or narrativity with Jesus Mary Joseph at the door
to greet the wee three kings of ore

Pause

you're neither here nor there you're past the point of no return and
what's the point you've gone to giving off a smell of camphor carried
on and here's the carrion you're doing fine you've got the hang of
pomander with Sal or Sue who blew through who do you do look out
now the rest's to come before the next beat's drummed to spring a
trap that you'll fall into some or several times again alas a loss a lot a
little bit of seasoning will spice up all that dead meat heating on the
stove you never got to stop to turn off at the next exit and circle back
to where the thought occurred and lured you off the train that's
boarded up with cedar chest where clothes in mothballs wait the
winter out

This and That

It's not what I said, but what I meant to say about what I had to say
that should be said about what I meant was this: to say what I meant
about what I said I had to say that what I should have said was "I
meant to say it's not what I said but what I meant". It's not what I
meant, but what I said should be said about what I meant to say. I
mean I said what I meant. I said "what" but what I meant was "this"
— I mean what I said was "It's not what I said but what I meant to say
about what I said that was what I had to say about this." I mean, I
meant to say that — and what I meant to say about that is this. Not
that "that" is "this", but let's say it is, and what I mean to say is that
this is what I meant: "that". In other words, this.

SOLUTIONS

(The following poems and their titles derive from words occurring in solutions to cryptic crosswords in *The Penguin Book of Sunday Times Crosswords* [London: Penguin Books, 1975]. Occasional liberties have been taken in altering the grammatical forms of the solution-words, selectively repeating certain of them, and adding prepositions and connectives. Honesty compels me to admit that the words are not necessarily ones for which I solved the clues, though I did manage to get most of them.)

Board Residence

Evil-doing duck duelled ogres, naphtha silencing back-seat driver, sacra twisted, aged. Desireless Peruvians aped Portobello Naiad, lying. Slowest blank cartridge desists, disabusing hard-headed orgy. Deep-sea air-mail bedside reading.

Kettle Foliation

Obedient Lydia ports facelift. Hertford staircase tea-chest odours interest Landseer. Egg-nog rustler stalls passport knavery. Lastly, settlers defile demoted actuary, paint the town red, minsters by-passed. Negative volition.

Breeches

Missionaries eluded apostate hedonist. Erica shed a tear. Portland Bill shed a tear. Major Barbara shed a tear. Hamlet shed a tear. Nathaniel shed a tear. All, in vain, agree: minatory missionaries.

Isothermal Idiom

Castles in Spain incur increases. Hang the expense: dumping assures benefit. Offensive guru landscapes Treasure Island. Gascons, presenting arms, breathe, peel, hang the sash.

Hereat

Black stockings tangoed. Keats read the minutes. Utrillo read the spelling lesson. Chain-mail still tangoed. Madeline read the minutes. Relatives read the sterling silver black stockings emanate. Still. Stool. Lucifer, nearing Madeline, tangoed. Defenders emanate unnatural norms, derange Utrillo devaluing sterling silver, overstep summer. Still.

Social

Penelope Stuffs Director, "Atonal Amazon" Main Part
Stout-Hearted House-Warming
Unsigned Oppose Gringo Limerick, Denude Whistler
Paduan, Norman Lock Out Plot
Titania Fine
Arts Solitude Fathoms Beaker
Curates Shrugged Questions, Engaged Nippers, Dish

Dossier

Shrines buckled, Canterbury Tales plodded, Constable seduced sisters, sniper resided in sand-dunes, troops reposed. Sovereign states vague. Sten gun legal tonight. Scribe detests bathroom antiphon.

Salve

A history-book is perpetual. Elgar is a flash-in-the-pan, a drainpipe beyond measure, who slips tiaras to senators, dashes utensils on the ingle, ruminates with beady eye, and steals cacti from literati. He should be executed in Fleet Street by an irate operative of barbarous aspect.

Telegram

Come back, Toffee. Tonga miserable. All right: punish. Others tripe. Embers Hotel. Cable.

Editor for the press: Christopher Dewdney
Cover design: Gordon Robertson
Cover image: from *The Plastic Typewriter* by Paul Dutton
Author photograph: Brian Fawcett

COACH HOUSE PRESS
401 (rear) Huron Street
Toronto, Canada M5S 2G5